Toppers

SMALL QUILTS TO ACCENT ANY DECOR

Lynda Milligan & Nancy Smith

POSSIBILITIES

Publishers of DreamSpinners® patterns, I'll Teach Myself®
sewing products, and Possibilities® books...

Acknowledgements

We would like to take this opportunity to thank the staff of our retail store, Great American Quilt Factory, and our accounting department for their enthusiasm and inspiration. Thank you, Judy Carpenter, for all you do, which is a lot of everything. Because of you we have the latest fabric and notions to use in our designs. Thanks, Chris Scott, for checking in and marking everything that comes through the back door. Ginny Rogliano is the best store manager we could have. We marvel at your ability to remember customers' names and the projects they are working on as well as keeping the store running smoothly.

Thank you, Ruth Haggbloom and Terri Wiley, two long-time employees who have been with us through good times and bad. You've been an invaluable part of our quilt family. If you have had any photo transfers made though our company, they were probably done by Sharron Shimbel, our own Australian quilter who keeps us knowledgeable about quilting 'down under'. Thanks to Courtney Collier who helps check merchandise in and very willingly cuts Nancy's or Lynda's vintage fabric into fat quarters.

Jean Denton, Anita Springer, and Maggie Thomas are always ready with friendly advice and a quick smile or laugh to brighten your day. Thanks also to Carolyn Schmitt, Ann Petersen, Gwinn Downton, and Sandi Fruehling for taking on quilting or piecing jobs in spite of your own hectic days. To our newest employees, Kathie Gibbons, Denise Ramsburg, Diana Leher and Susan Auskaps, we thank you for your fresh outlook on quilting and your enthusiasm. Last, but not least we thank Marie Gifford and Tawnya Romig-Foster for filling in when you are needed. We owe all of you a great big, huge thank-you for keeping our retail store among the best in the country.

Thanks to Jan Albee, Jan Hagan, and Sara Felton for ordering, shipping, and marketing. They make sure the books get to you. Thanks to Aina Martin for paying the bills and getting our paychecks to us!

A special thank-you to Marilyn Robinson for her assistance in photo styling and Alissa Crowley, Joanne Patton and Marilyn Robinson for letting us photograph quilts in their lovely homes.

Nancy and Lynda

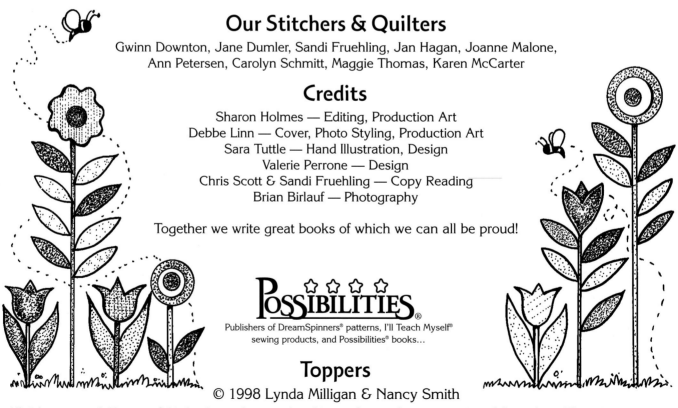

Our Stitchers & Quilters

Gwinn Downton, Jane Dumler, Sandi Fruehling, Jan Hagan, Joanne Malone, Ann Petersen, Carolyn Schmitt, Maggie Thomas, Karen McCarter

Credits

Sharon Holmes — Editing, Production Art
Debbe Linn — Cover, Photo Styling, Production Art
Sara Tuttle — Hand Illustration, Design
Valerie Perrone — Design
Chris Scott & Sandi Fruehling — Copy Reading
Brian Birlauf — Photography

Together we write great books of which we can all be proud!

POSSIBILITIES®

Publishers of DreamSpinners® patterns, I'll Teach Myself® sewing products, and Possibilities® books...

Toppers

Table of Contents

 # Introduction

HOW A BOOK IDEA IS BORN

We design and make an incredible number of quilts every year for publication in our books, but they usually are visiting other stores, and very seldom do we get to take them home. One day, while contemplating this and thinking how nice it would be to have a different quilt on our bed for each season or holiday, we came up with the idea of Toppers.

Toppers were, to us, small quilts that you could put over another simpler quilt to change the look. It would either be rectangular to go over the pillows like a sham or square to be placed on the bed diagonally. Because they were much smaller, the chances of us getting them made were much greater. We could have a different topper for Christmas, Halloween, spring and a extra-special one for a special day. The underneath quilt would be made with eight-inch squares and be quilted by machine.

The more we talked, the more ideas we had for the Toppers. They could be used on the back of a couch or on an overstuffed chair. They could be used on the table as a runner or on the back of a bed for a unique headboard idea. The ideas were coming fast and furiously. As usual, we started making our Toppers and had trouble deciding when to stop. We had in our minds separate books for pillow sham Toppers, couch Toppers, table Toppers, and so on. We finally decided to incorporate several ideas into one book. We know that you, too, will think of other ways to use Toppers, and then you will be able to change your bedroom decor with your mood or with the season. As we are writing this, it is the last day of summer, and we haven't started our autumn toppers yet. Better go!

NEWFANGLED NOTIONS & METHODS

Piecing, applique, and quilting methods are changing with the inventions of new notions and techniques. If you have been quilting for several years, you undoubtedly remember plastic and sandpaper templates and cutting everything individually with scissors. I often think that new quilters should have to take a class in the old techniques just so they appreciate how far quilting has come. But then I realize that is how so many of the 'do it by hand only' quilters felt about the new 'but I can do it faster and better by machine' quilters. To keep up on the newest methods, check out your local quilt shop, take classes, and read current books and magazines.

Each time we write a book, we have to decide whether to incorporate the newest techniques or not. Unless the technique or notion has been around awhile and is widely available, we usually don't use it. But feel free to incorporate them yourself. For example, Triangles on a Roll and Thangles are paper triangles printed on tear-away paper that make piecing right-angle triangles incredibly fast and accurate. Be sure to check them out and adjust your yardage as needed.

Supplies that you will need that are not included in the yardage charts are fusible web if you are using that technique for your applique, and the batting to finish your quilt. There are several types of fusible web, and you will find that your fabric store will probably have their own preference. If you like a particular brand, keep about a two-yard supply on hand. Keep the instruction sheet as there are many differences in the bonding techniques. Our applique patterns have been **reversed** for fusible web applique. If you choose to hand applique, you will want to reverse them again.

As far as batting goes, there are many great battings to use for quilting. Some are easier to quilt by hand, and others make it easier to quilt by machine. Some are fluffy, some are very flat. Check with your local fabric shop to see what the preferences are for the type of quilting you will be doing. Note your quilt size so that you can buy the yardage or the proper size of prepackaged batting.

YOU, TOO, CAN BE A DESIGNER

We have shown most of the Toppers in one size only but have listed yardage and sizes for twin, double/queen, and king. You will generally only have to add a few more pieced blocks, make the background larger, and spread out or add more applique pieces. Use the yardage requirements to help you estimate yardage when changing a design. For example, use the twin size yardage on the Stars & Holly Topper to estimate how much to buy for the square one.

Feel free to substitute a different block in the patchwork Toppers. Find a block or design a block that is the same size as the one you are replacing. You could also substitute an applique block of your choice. Instead of placing the blocks side-by-side, piece them into one of the square Toppers.

Have fun changing colors on any of the Toppers. Our Stars and Holly Topper could easily become your Patriotic Star Topper by eliminating the holly and using red, white, and blue fabrics. Enjoy exercising your creativity with these Toppers and be sure to send us photos of how you are using them.

HOW TO USE TOPPERS

Bed toppers can go over the pillows either way—with the opening to the front *or* the back. We call the part of the Topper that goes under the pillow the underlay. Bed Toppers also look very nice folded at the foot of the bed. When using a Topper on a couch or a chair, the underlay falls over the back to help keep the Topper in place. If you want to make a Topper into a wall hanging, simply leave off the underlay. In addition, finishing the pillows with binding makes it possible to use them for wall hangings. We are sure you will have many more ideas for using our patterns! Happy stitching!

Big Square & Reversible Quilts

Sideways view of double/queen size

Photo pages given with specific quilts on page 7. These quilts are "comforter" size—that is, they cover the mattress only, and they go *under* the pillows.

Use 42-44″ wide fabric. When strips appear in the cutting list, cut crossgrain strips (selvage to selvage).

	LAP	**TWIN**	**DOUBLE/QUEEN**	**KING**
Size width by length	48x72″	64x88″	88x96″	104x96″
8″ Squares Set	6x9	8x11	11x12	13x12
Total # of Squares	54	88	132	156

Yardage

	LAP	**TWIN**	**DOUBLE/QUEEN**	**KING**
Scraps at least 9″ square	54	88	132	156
OR yardage to total	3¾ yds.	5¾ yds.	8½ yds.	10 yds.
Backing (vertical piecing)	4⅝ yds.	5½ yds.	8¾ yds.	8¾ yds.
Binding	⅝ yd.	⅔ yd.	⅞ yd.	⅞ yd.

Cutting

	LAP	**TWIN**	**DOUBLE/QUEEN**	**KING**
Squares – 8½″	54	88	132	156
Binding – 2½″ strips	7	8	10	11

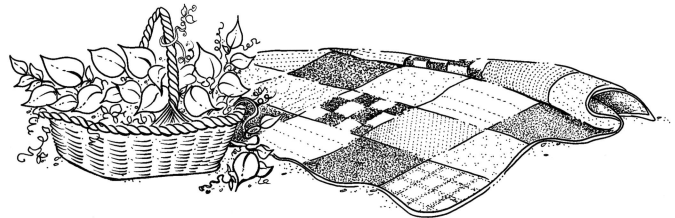

Big Square Quilt Directions

Use ¼″ seam allowance throughout.

1. For lap size quilt, stitch squares into 9 horizontal rows of 6. See chart for layouts of other sizes.

2. Stitch rows together. Press well.

3. For lap or twin quilt, cut two backing pieces 4-6″ longer than quilt top and piece vertically. For double/queen and king, cut three backing pieces 4-6″ longer than quilt top and piece vertically.

4. Use your favorite layering, quilting, and binding methods to finish quilt.

DENIM BLUES QUILT Photo on page 32

Four-patches are substituted for nine of the squares and scattered randomly.

HOMESPUN WARMTH QUILT Photo on page 57

Made with the standard setting of 8″ squares.

WINTER BRIGHTS QUILT Photo on page 20

One black fabric is substituted for alternating squares. Purchase a piece of black fabric that is slightly more than one-half the given yardage for the squares.

FLANNEL FUN QUILT Photo on page 21

Made with the standard setting of 8″ squares.

NORTHERN NIGHTS QUILT

Photos on pages 25 & 64

Four-patches are substituted for nine of the squares and scattered randomly.

Reversible Quilt Directions

To make reversible, whole-cloth quilts, buy the same amount of fabric for the front as listed in the chart for the backing. Be sure to allow extra if matching large plaids or buffalo checks. To offset the seams on the lap or twin quilt, split one of the front pieces into two side panels. Adjust width of center panel as desired. Stitch side panels to center panel. Repeat with pieces for backing. (Seams for the double/queen and king quilts are already offset because they require three panels.) Trim outside edges of top and backing to desired quilt size plus 4-6″ in both directions. Quilt as desired. Trim raw edges to desired quilt size. Bind.

GREEN PLAID QUILT Photo on page 29

SOUTHWEST QUILT Photo on page 17

LINEN CHECKS QUILT Photo on page 28

Example layout with four-patch blocks added

Moss Rose Topper

Photo on page 53. Twin size has three blocks, double/queen size has four blocks, and king size has five blocks.

Use 42-44" wide fabric. When strips appear in the cutting list, cut cross-grain strips (selvage to selvage).

	TWIN	DOUBLE/QUEEN	KING
Size width by height	55x40"	70x40"	85x40"
Number of 15" Blocks	3	4	5

Yardage

	TWIN	DOUBLE/QUEEN	KING
Blocks			
dark	¾ yd.	1 yd.	1⅛ yds.
medium 1 (corners)	¼ yd.	¼ yd.	¼ yd.
medium 2 (interior)	¼ yd.	¼ yd.	¼ yd.
light	⅝ yd.	⅝ yd.	¾ yd.
Border 1	⅓ yd.	⅓ yd.	⅜ yd.
Border 2	⅝ yd.	⅔ yd.	¾ yd.
Underlay	1⅛ yds.	1⅛ yds.	1⅝ yds.
Backing	1⅞ yds.	2¼ yds.	2⅝ yds.
Binding	½ yd.	½ yd.	⅝ yd.

Cutting

	TWIN	DOUBLE/QUEEN	KING
A – dark – 4" squares	3	4	5
B – light – 3⅜" squares	*24	*32	*40
B – medium 1 – 3⅜" sqs.	*6	*8	*10
B – dark – 3⅜" squares	*12	*16	*20
C – light – 6¼" squares	**3	**4	**5
C – medium 2 – 6¼" sqs.	**3	**4	**5
C – dark – 6¼" squares	**6	**8	**10
D – dark – 3" squares	12	16	20
Border 1 – 2" strips	4	4	5
Border 2 – 4" strips	4	5	6
Binding – 2½" strips	5	6	7

*Cut these squares in half diagonally to make triangles.

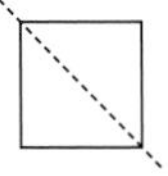

**Cut these squares in quarters diagonally to make triangles.

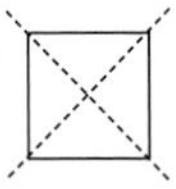

Directions

Use ¼″ seam allowance throughout.

1. Piece blocks as shown.

2. Stitch blocks into a horizontal row. Press well.

3. Take vertical measurement of block row. Cut two Border 1 strips this length and stitch to sides. Press. Measure width of row. Prepare two Border 1 strips this length and stitch to top and bottom.

4. Repeat Step 3 for Border 2. Press well.

5. Piece underlay with vertical seam(s). It should measure 16″ vertically and be the same width as your Topper. Stitch underlay to Topper.

6. Use your favorite layering, quilting, and binding methods to finish Topper.

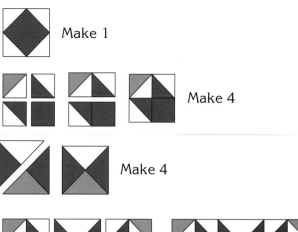

Make 1

Make 4

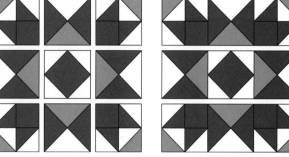

Make 4

14″ Pillow
Broderie perse applique.
Photo on page 53.

9

North Woods Topper

Twin size

Photo on page 57. To adjust design for double/queen and king toppers, spread and/or add applique pieces.

Use 42-44" wide fabric. When strips appear in the cutting list, cut cross-grain strips (selvage to selvage).

	TWIN	DOUBLE/QUEEN	KING
Size width by height	48x40"	70x40"	86x40"

Yardage

Appliques – scraps up to 9x18"

	TWIN	DOUBLE/QUEEN	KING
Sky	1⅜ yds.	2 yds.	2½ yds.
Ground	1⅜ yds.	2 yds.	2½ yds.
Border	½ yd.	½ yd.	⅝ yd.
Backing	1¾ yds.	2⅜ yds.	2⅞ yds.
Binding	½ yd.	½ yd.	⅝ yd.

Cutting Patterns on pages 72-77

Applique pieces
  as desired

	TWIN	DOUBLE/QUEEN	KING
Sky	44x29½"	66x29½"	82x29½"
Ground	44x7"	66x7"	82x7"
Border – 2½" strips	5	6	7
Binding – 2½" strips	5	6	7

Directions

Use ¼″ seam allowance throughout.

1. Stitch ground piece to sky piece. Press.

2. Measure height of background and cut side borders this length. Stitch to background. Press. Measure width of Topper and prepare top/bottom borders this length. Stitch to Topper. Press.

3. Applique center of Topper with your favorite method. Press lightly.

4. Use your favorite layering, quilting, and binding methods to finish Topper.

16″ Pillow
Photo on page 57.

16x43″ Chairback
Photo on page 57.

Example of adjusted design for double/queen Topper

Northern Neighbors Topper

Twin size

Photo on page 64 (also shown folded on page 57). To adjust design for double/queen and king toppers, spread and/or add applique pieces.

Use 42-44″ wide fabric. When strips appear in the cutting list, cut cross-grain strips (selvage to selvage).

	TWIN	DOUBLE/QUEEN	KING
Size width by height	48x40″	70x40″	86x40″

Yardage

	TWIN	DOUBLE/QUEEN	KING
Appliques – scraps up to 8x13″			
Background (sky)	1½ yds.	2⅛ yds.	2½ yds.
Hill	1½ yds.	2⅛ yds.	2½ yds.
Border – scraps over 3x5½″to total	1 yd.	1⅛ yds.	1¼ yds.
Backing	1¾ yds.	2⅜ yds.	2⅞ yds.
Binding	½ yd.	½ yd.	⅝ yd.

Cutting Patterns on pages 62-69

	TWIN	DOUBLE/QUEEN	KING
Applique pieces as desired			
Sky	43x35″	65x35″	81x35″
Hill	43x12″	65x12″	81x12″
Border pieces – 3″ wide by 2½-5½″ long	45-55	65-75	75-85
Binding – 2½″ strips	5	6	7

Directions

Use ¼" seam allowance throughout.

1. Back hill piece with fusible web. Mark a hilly line along top edge on wrong side then cut on line. Fuse hill to background (sky).

2. Stitch border rectangles together in random order into two side units and two top/bottom units (see lengths below). Stitch side borders to sky/hill piece first, then top and bottom borders.

   - **Twin:** side units 35", top and bottom units 48"
   - **Double/queen:** side units 35", top and bottom units 70"
   - **King:** side units 35", top and bottom units 86"

3. Applique center of Topper with your favorite method. Press. Use black permanent marking pen to make eyes and mouths of snowmen.

4. Use your favorite layering, quilting, and binding methods to finish Topper.

Example of adjusted design for double/queen Topper

Kokopelli Topper

Twin size

Photo on page 17. To adjust design for double/queen and king toppers, spread and/or add applique pieces.

Use 42-44″ wide fabric. When strips appear in the cutting list, cut cross-grain strips (selvage to selvage).

	Twin	**Double/Queen**	**King**
Size width by height	49x40″	70x40″	84x40″

Yardage

Appliques – scraps up to 9x15″			
Background	1½ yds.	2 yds.	2½ yds.
Border (inner)	⅝ yd.	¾ yd.	¾ yd.
Border (center)	⅝ yd.	¾ yd.	¾ yd.
Border (outer)	¾ yd.	⅞ yd.	⅞ yd.
Underlay	1¼ yds.	1¼ yds.	1⅝ yds.
Backing	1⅝ yds.	2¼ yds.	2⅝ yds.
Binding	½ yd.	½ yd.	⅝ yd.

Cutting Patterns on pages 70-72

		Twin	Double/Queen	King
Applique pieces as desired				
Background (will trim to fit)		44x20″	65x20″	78x20″
Border (inner)	3½″ strips	2	3	3
	2¼″ strips	2	3	3
Border (center)	1¾″ strips	2	3	3
	4¼″ strips	2	3	3
Border (outer)	3½″ strips	2	3	3
	2¼″ strips	2	3	3
	4¾″ square	1	1	1
Binding – 2½″ strips		5	6	7

Directions

Use ¼″ seam allowance throughout.

Border diagrams on page 16.

1. Border Patchwork

   a. For twin, make two Strip Set A and two Strip Set B. For double/queen and king, make three sets each of A and B. Press seam allowances of Set A **out** from center, and seam allowances of B **in** toward center. Crosscut into 1¾″ segments.

   b. Stitch pairs of segments together as shown (see below for how many). Stitch pairs into rows for top border, bottom border, and each side border. See diagram. Press seam allowances carefully in one direction.

      • **Twin:** 38 pairs of segments
        13 pairs each for top and bottom borders
        6 pairs for each side border

      • **Double/queen:** 50 pairs of segments
        19 pairs each for top and bottom borders
        6 pairs for each side border

      • **King:** 58 pairs of segments
        23 pairs each for top and bottom borders
        6 pairs for each side border

   c. Trim long edges, leaving ¼″ seam allowance, as shown.

   d. Cut 4¾″ outer border fabric square in quarters diagonally. Stitch one of the resulting triangles to the left end of each border piece as shown. Trim end of each strip even with triangle.

2. Measure top and bottom border strips from seam intersection to seam intersection as shown. Repeat with side border strips. Cut down the background rectangle to these measurements plus ½″ for seam allowances. For example (twin size), if top and bottom borders measure 42″ and sides measure 17″, cut down the background rectangle to 42½x17½″.

3. Stitch borders to Topper, starting and stopping at seam intersections. Stitch diagonal corner seams.

4. Applique center of Topper with your favorite method, making cactus and kokopelli pieces face as desired. Press.

5. Piece underlay with vertical seam(s). It should measure 16″ vertically and be the same width as your Topper. Stitch underlay to Topper.

6. Use your favorite layering, quilting, and binding methods to finish Topper. We outline quilted the appliques and crosshatched the background and border.

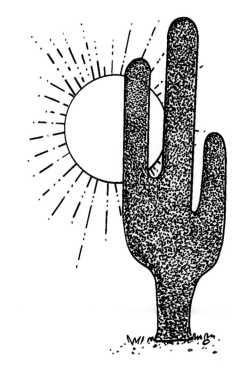

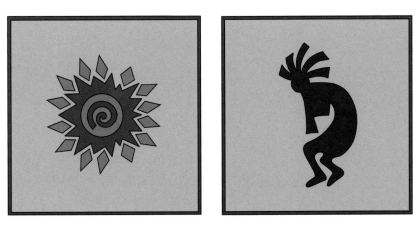

16″ Pillows. Photo on page 17.

Border Diagrams for Kokopelli Topper

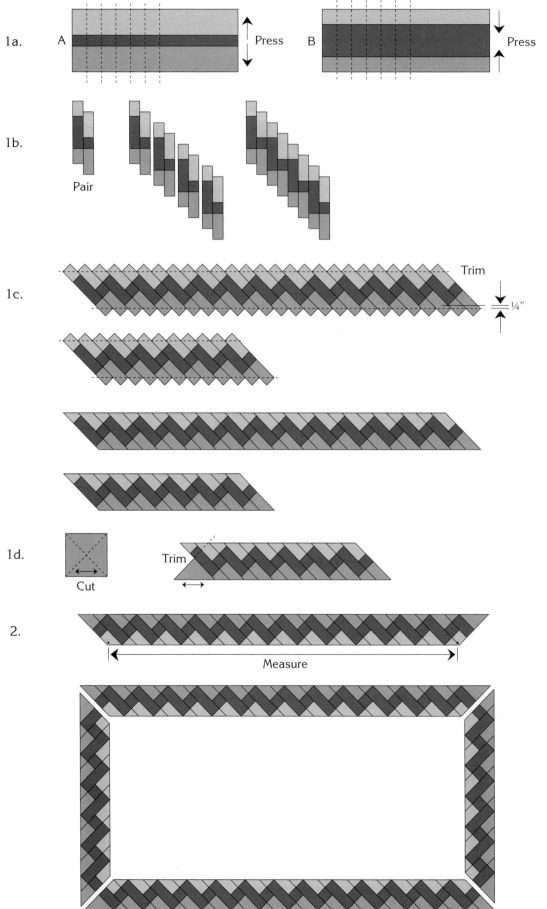

1a. A   Press   B   Press

1b.   Pair

1c.   Trim   ¼"

1d.   Cut   Trim

2.   Measure

Frosty Flannels Topper

Twin size

Photo on page 21. To adjust design for double/queen and king toppers, spread and/or add applique pieces.

Use 42-44″ wide fabric. When strips appear in the cutting list, cut cross-grain strips (selvage to selvage).

	TWIN	DOUBLE/QUEEN	KING
Size width by height	48x40″	70x40″	86x40″

Yardage

	TWIN	DOUBLE/QUEEN	KING
Appliques – scraps up to 7½″ square			
Background	1½ yds.	2 yds.	2½ yds.
Border – scraps over 3x5½″ to total	1 yd.	1⅛ yds.	1¼ yds.
Backing	1¾ yds.	2⅓ yds.	2⅞ yds.
Binding	½ yd.	½ yd.	⅝ yd.

Cutting Patterns on pages 78-79

	TWIN	DOUBLE/QUEEN	KING
Applique pieces as desired			
Background	43x35″	65x35″	81x35″
Border pieces – 3″ wide by 3½-5½″ long	40-50	50-60	60-70
Binding – 2½″ strips	5	6	7

Directions

Use ¼″ seam allowance throughout.

1. Stitch border rectangles together in random order into two side units and two top/bottom units (see lengths below). Stitch side borders to background piece first, then top and bottom borders.

   • **Twin:** side units 35″, top and bottom units 48″

   • **Double/queen:** side units 35″, top and bottom units 70″

   • **King:** side units 35″, top and bottom units 86″

2. Applique center of Topper with your favorite method. Reverse some of the faces for variety, if desired. Applique eyes and mouths or use black permanent marking pen. Press.

3. Use your favorite layering, quilting, and binding methods to finish Topper.

Don't save this colorful quilt and Topper just for birthdays. Make small occasions into celebrations—a great report card, perfect attendance, the first day of school, a new job, retirement, a team or sports win, a prom date, a first-time driver's license, the school play, Mother's Day, or Father's Day.

Celebration Topper

Twin size

Photo on page 20. To adjust design for double/queen and king toppers, spread and/or add applique pieces. For the banner, background was cut 54x24″ and a casing was added to the back for hanging. Photo on page 61.

Use 42-44″ wide fabric. When strips appear in the cutting list, cut cross-grain strips (selvage to selvage).

	TWIN	DOUBLE/QUEEN	KING
Size width by height	48x40″	70x40″	86x40″

Yardage

Appliques – scraps up to 8x9″

	TWIN	DOUBLE/QUEEN	KING
Background	1⅝ yds.	2¼ yds.	2⅝ yds.
Backing	1¾ yds.	2⅜ yds.	2⅞ yds.
Binding	½ yd.	½ yd.	⅝ yd.
Edging – scraps over 6″ sq.	11	16	20

Cutting Patterns on pages 51-59

Applique pieces as desired

	TWIN	DOUBLE/QUEEN	KING
Background	48x40″	70x40″	86x40″
Binding – 2½″ strips	5	6	7
Edging – 6″ squares	11	16	20

Directions

Use ¼" seam allowance throughout.

1. Applique center of Topper with your favorite method. Press lightly.

2. Use your favorite layering and quilting methods. Trim backing and batting even with top.

3. Prairie Point Edging

   a. Fold and press prairie points for edging as shown.

   b. Pin and then baste prairie points to bottom edge of Topper, slipping one inside the other as needed to space them evenly.

   c. Prepare a strip of binding slightly longer than width of Topper. Fold binding strip wrong sides together and stitch to right side of bottom edge of Topper. Fold binding strip all the way to the back of the quilt so that prairie points stick out at the edge. Hand stitch folded edge of binding to back of quilt. One inch of binding will show on the back along this edge.

   d. Stitch binding strips to sides and top of Topper, mitering at top corners, and leaving ½" extending at bottom corners. Wrap extensions around bottom corners, then fold binding to stitching line on back. Hand stitch in place.

3a.

3b.

Example layouts for 14x18" place mats. Photo on page 61.

24   Stars & Holly Topper , Stars & Holly Square Topper

Log Cabin Topper

Twin size

Photo on page 25. Twin size has three blocks, double/queen size has five blocks, and king size has seven blocks.

Use 42-44″ wide fabric. When strips appear in the cutting list, cut cross-grain strips (selvage to selvage).

	TWIN	DOUBLE/QUEEN	KING
Size width by height	48x40″	68x40″	88x40″
Number of 10″ Blocks	3	5	7

Yardage

	TWIN	DOUBLE/QUEEN	KING
Light scraps for blocks & sawtooth border – to total	1¾ yds.	2½ yds.	2¾ yds.
Lights for log cabin border – ⅛ yd. pieces	5	5	5
Dark scraps for blocks, corner squares in log cabin borders, & triangles in sawtooth borders – to total	1 yd.	1⅜ yds.	1⅝ yds.
Darks for log cabin border – ⅛ yd. pieces	5	10	10
Appliques – scraps at least 6x8″			
Outside border	½ yd.	½ yd.	½ yd.
Underlay	1 yd.	1 yd.	1⅓ yds.
Backing	1¾ yds.	2⅓ yds.	2⅞ yds.
Binding	½ yd.	½ yd.	⅝ yd.

Cutting Patterns on page 48

For blocks			
Lights – 3″ square	12	20	28
5½″ square	3	5	7
3⅜″ square	*12	*20	*28
Darks – 3⅜″ square	*12	*20	*28
Applique stars & hearts	3 each	5 each	7 each
Log cabin border			
Lights – 1½″ strips	10	10	10
Darks – 1½″ squares	20	20	20
1½″ strips	10	20	20
Sawtooth border			
Lights – 2½″ squares	4	4	4
2⅞″ squares	*30	*40	*50
Darks – 2⅞″ squares	*30	*40	*50
Outside border – 2½″ strips	4	6	6
Binding – 2½″ strips	5	6	7

*Cut these squares in half diagonally to make triangles.

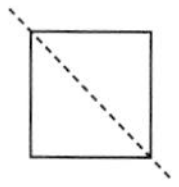

Directions

Use ¼″ seam allowance throughout.

1. Piece blocks as shown. Applique hearts and stars to centers of blocks using your favorite method. Reverse directions of pieces as desired.

2. Stitch blocks into a horizontal row. Press well.

3. Measure height and width of block row. Prepare two light log cabin strips (the height measurement) and two dark log cabin strips (the width measurement). Stitch 1½″ squares to ends of top and bottom border strips. Stitch side border strips on first, then top and bottom border strips. Press.

4. Repeat Step 3 four times to complete the log cabin stripping. Press well.

5. Make half-square triangle units for sawtooth border. Stitch together into side and top/bottom borders with 2½″ squares added to ends of top/bottom borders. Stitch side borders on first, then top and bottom. Adjust to fit by taking up or letting out a few of the seams between units.

- **Twin:** 60 units, 10 for each side and 20 for top and bottom (light/dark reversed at center)

- **Double/queen:** 80 units, 10 for each side and 30 for top and bottom (light/dark reversed at center)

- **King:** 100 units, 10 for each side and 40 for top and bottom (light/dark reversed at center)

6. Press well. Measure height of Topper and prepare two outside borders this measurement. Stitch to sides of Topper. Press. Measure width of Topper and prepare top and bottom borders this measurement. Stitch to top and bottom of Topper. Press.

7. Piece underlay with vertical seam(s). It should measure 12½″ vertically and be the same width as your Topper. Stitch underlay to Topper.

8. Use your favorite layering, quilting, and binding methods to finish Topper.

1.

For each block:

Make 8   Make 4

5.

For border:

Make units reverse at center

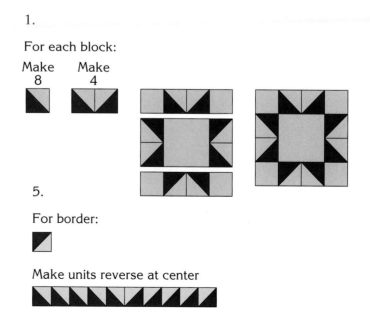

Plaid Posies Topper, Linen Checks Quilt

Rolling Star Topper

Double/queen size

Photo on page 29. Twin size has two blocks, double/queen size has three blocks, and king size has four blocks.

Use 42-44″ wide fabric. When strips appear in the cutting list, cut cross-grain strips (selvage to selvage).

	TWIN	DOUBLE/QUEEN	KING
Size width by height	45½x40″	64¾x40″	84x40″
Number of 19¼″ Blocks	2	3	4

Yardage

Center diamonds	½ yd.	⅝ yd.	¾ yd.
Outer diamonds	½ yd.	⅝ yd.	¾ yd.
Squares	½ yd.	⅝ yd.	¾ yd.
Triangles	⅜ yd.	⅜ yd.	⅝ yd.
Border 1	¼ yd.	¼ yd.	⅓ yd.
Border 2	⅝ yd.	⅔ yd.	¾ yd.
Underlay	1 yd.	1 yd.	1½ yds.
Backing	1¾ yds.	2¼ yds.	2¾ yds.
Binding	½ yd.	½ yd.	⅝ yd.

Cutting Pattern on page 69

Center diamonds	16	24	32
Outer diamonds	16	24	32
Squares – 4½″	16	24	32
Triangles – 6½″ squares	*4	*6	*8
Border 1 – 1½″ strips	3	4	5
Border 2 – 3″ strips	4	5	6
Binding – 2½″ strips	5	6	7

*Cut these squares in half diagonally to make triangles.

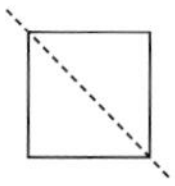

Directions

Use ¼″ seam allowance throughout.

1. Piece blocks as shown. All pieces except corner triangles are set in; stitch to seam intersections only, not to cut edges.

2. Stitch blocks into a horizontal row. Press well.

3. Measure height of block row. Cut two Border 1 strips this length and stitch to sides. Press. Measure width of row. Prepare two Border 1 strips this length and stitch to top and bottom.

4. Repeat Step 3 for Border 2. Press well.

5. Piece underlay with vertical seam(s). It should measure 14″ vertically and be the same width as your Topper. Stitch underlay to Topper.

6. Use your favorite layering, quilting, and binding methods to finish Topper.

1.
For each block:

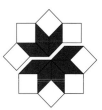

Make 4

19″ Pillow
Photo on page 29.

Throw Pillows

Throw pillows make a great addition to any bed or couch ensemble. The pillow covers in our photos were all made with an envelope back and a bound edge. General directions follow for these two techniques that apply to all pillow sizes.

Purchase backing and binding yardage based on the size of your pillow. Pillow forms are available in even-numbered sizes such as 14″, 16″, and so on, or you can make your own. A snug fit is best, and it can be achieved by making a cover that is ″ smaller than the form, or by wrapping a too-small form with a layer of batting to fill out the cover.

Use the first steps of the Topper directions for making blocks and the captions under the pillow diagrams (at the end of the directions section for each Topper) for adding borders. Quilt as desired before adding envelope back and binding.

Envelope Back

Cut two backing pieces the same size as the pillow top. Hem one side of each with a 1″ double-folded and topstitched hem. Press. Lay pillow backing pieces wrong sides up, overlapping the hemmed edges 4″ to create the opening for the envelope back. Increase overlap for very large pillow covers. Center wrong side of pillow top over backing pieces and trim away excess backing on each side. Pin and then baste entire outside edge of pillow cover with a ¼″ seam allowance.

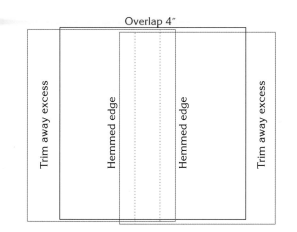

Binding

Prepare a length of binding from strips cut 2½″ wide; it should be 8-9″ longer than the perimeter of the pillow cover. Press open any seam allowances. Starting in the center of one side and leaving a 4″ tail of binding unstitched at the beginning, stitch binding strip to pillow with a ⅜″ seam allowance, mitering corners as shown. Stop 4-5″ from where stitching began and take out of machine. Lay loose ends of binding over each other along remaining part of seamline. Trim ends so they overlap ½″. Stitch ends of binding right sides together with a ¼″ seam allowance (bunch up the pillow cover as needed). Finger-press the seam allowance open, refold the binding and finish stitching it to the pillow cover. Hand stitch folded edge of binding to back of pillow cover along stitching line, folding miters at corners as shown to distribute the bulk.

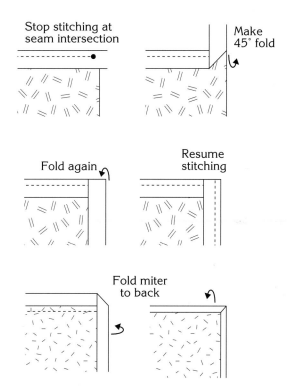

Frosty Topper

Twin size

Photo on page 49. To adjust design for double/queen and king toppers, spread and/or add applique pieces.

Use 42-44″ wide fabric. When strips appear in the cutting list, cut cross-grain strips (selvage to selvage).

	TWIN	DOUBLE/QUEEN	KING
Size width by height	48x40″	70x40″	86x40″

Yardage

Appliques – scraps up to 7½″ square

Background	1⅝ yds.	2¼ yds.	2⅝ yds.
Backing	1¾ yds.	2⅓ yds.	2⅞ yds.
Binding	½ yd.	½ yd.	⅝ yd.
Edging – scraps over 6″ sq.	11	16	20

Cutting Patterns on pages 78-79

Applique pieces as desired

Background	48x40″	70x40″	86x40″
Binding – 2½″ strips	5	6	7
Edging – 6″ squares	11	16	20

Directions

Use ¼″ seam allowance throughout.

1. Applique center of Topper with your favorite method. Reverse some of the faces for variety, if desired. Applique eyes and mouths or use black permanent marking pen. Press.

2. Use your favorite layering and quilting methods. Trim backing and batting even with top.

3. Prairie Point Edging

   a. Fold and press prairie points for edging as shown.

   b. Pin and then baste prairie points to bottom edge of Topper, slipping one inside the other as needed to space them evenly.

   c. Prepare a strip of binding slightly longer than width of Topper. Fold binding strip wrong sides together and stitch to right side of bottom edge of Topper. Fold binding strip all the way to the back of the quilt so that prairie points stick out at the edge. Hand stitch folded edge of binding to back of quilt. One inch of binding will show on the back along this edge.

   d. Stitch binding strips to sides and top of Topper, mitering at top corners, and leaving ½″ extending at bottom corners. Wrap extensions around bottom corners, then fold binding to stitching line on back. Hand stitch in place.

3a.

3b.

Example layouts for 16″ pillows. Background is a large four-patch. Photo on page 49.

Plaid Posies Topper

Double/queen size

Photo on page 28. Adjust design for twin size by deleting applique pieces and for king size by spreading and/or adding applique pieces.

Use 42-44″ wide fabric. When strips appear in the cutting list, cut cross-grain strips (selvage to selvage).

	TWIN	DOUBLE/QUEEN	KING
Size width by height	48x46″	66x46″	82x46″

Yardage

Flowers & leaves scraps up to 5x6″			
Stems	⅛ yd.	⅛ yd.	⅙ yd.
Background	1½ yds.	2 yds.	2½ yds.
Border – scraps to total	⅞ yd.	1 yd.	1⅛ yds.
Backing	2⅝ yds.	2⅝ yds.	2⅝ yds.
Binding	½ yd.	½ yd.	⅝ yd.

Cutting Patterns on page 50

Applique pieces as desired (see directions for stems)			
Background	44½x42½″	62½x42½″	78½x42½″
Border – 2½″ squares	90	108	124
Binding – 2½″ strips	5	6	7

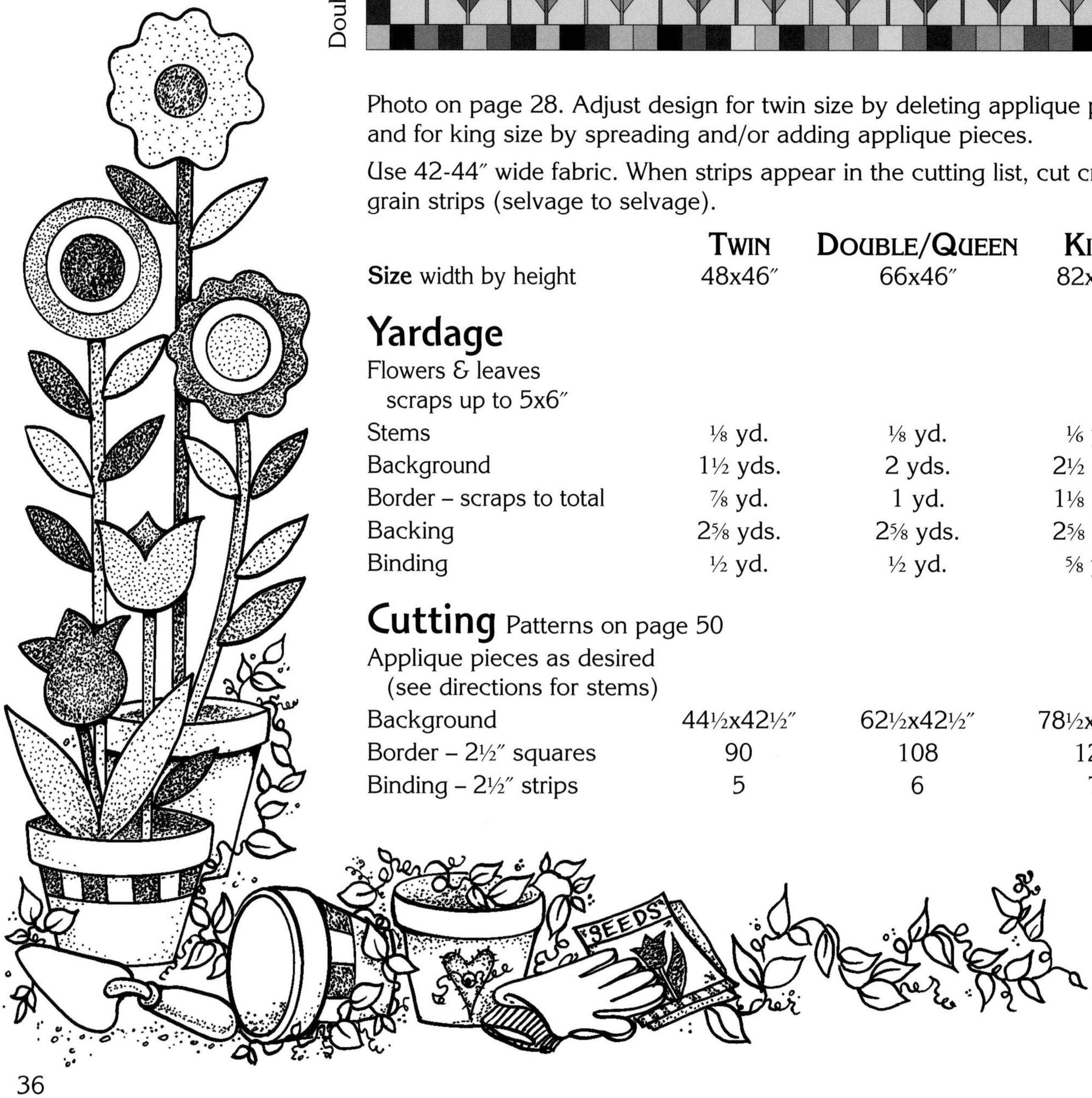

Directions

Use ¼″ seam allowance throughout.

1. Borders

    a. Stitch squares together (see below for how many) into two side borders and two top/bottom borders. Press.

    - **Twin:** 21 squares for each side border, 24 squares for top and bottom borders

    - **Double/queen:** 21 squares for each side border, 33 squares for top and bottom borders

    - **King:** 21 squares for each side border, 41 squares for top and bottom borders

    b. Stitch side borders to background rectangle, then top and bottom borders.

    c. Press well.

2. Applique center of Topper with your favorite method. The stems finish at ¼″ wide and are 4″, 11″, and 14″ in length in our sample. Press lightly.

3. Use your favorite layering, quilting, and binding methods to finish Topper.

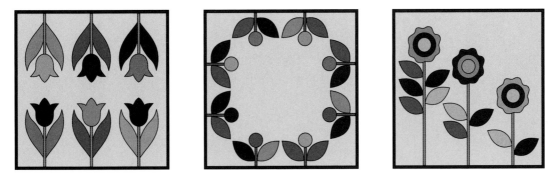

Example layouts for 16″ pillows. Photo on page 28.

Bear's Paw Topper

Double/queen size

Photo on page 32. Twin size has three blocks, double/queen size has five blocks, and king size has six blocks.

Use 42-44″ wide fabric. When strips appear in the cutting list, cut cross-grain strips (selvage to selvage).

	TWIN	DOUBLE/QUEEN	KING
Size width by height	52½x40″	76½x40″	88½x40″
Number of 10½″ Blocks	3	5	6

Yardage

	TWIN	DOUBLE/QUEEN	KING
Block background	½ yd.	⅔ yd.	⅞ yd.
Block dark fabrics, stripping & sashing – ⅝ yd. pieces	3	5	6
Underlay	1⅛ yds.	1⅛ yds.	1½ yds.
Backing	1⅞ yds.	2½ yds.	2⅞ yds.
Binding	½ yd.	½ yd.	⅝ yd.

Cutting

	TWIN	DOUBLE/QUEEN	KING
Background – 2x5″ rectangle	12	20	24
2″ square	12	20	24
2⅜″ square	*24	*40	*48
For each block from each dark fabric – 3½″ square – 4			
2″ square – 1			
2⅜″ square – *8			
Binding – 2½″ strips	5	6	7

*Cut these squares in half diagonally to make triangles.

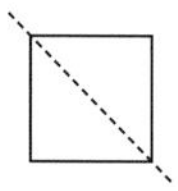

Directions

Use ¼″ seam allowance throughout.

1. Piece blocks as shown.

2. Stitch blocks into a horizontal row with sashing strips (cut size 2x11″) between blocks and at each end.

3. Prepare ten strips from extra dark fabrics for top and bottom of block row (see lengths below). Stitch strips into two sets of five. Trim to same width as block row. Stitch to top and bottom of block row. Press.
   - **Twin:** 2x40″
   - **Double/queen:** 2x63″
   - **King:** 2x75″

4. Prepare ten strips from extra dark fabrics for sides of block row that are 2x28″. Stitch strips into two sets of five. Trim to fit sides of block row. Stitch to sides of block row. Press.

5. Piece underlay with vertical seam(s). It should measure 15″ vertically and be the same width as your Topper. Stitch underlay to Topper.

6. Use your favorite layering, quilting, and binding methods to finish Topper.

For each block:

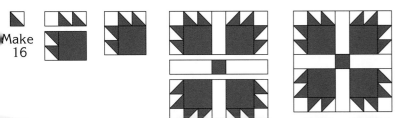

Make 16

16½″ Bear's Paw Pillow
Border made with 2″
strips & corner squares.
Photo on page 32.

15½″ Rail Fence Pillow
Made with leftover
2″ strips from Topper.
Photo on page 32.

39

Stars & Holly Topper

Double/queen size

Photo on page 24. Twin size has five blocks, double/queen size has seven blocks, and king size has eight blocks. For a great table runner, simply omit the underlay and cut Border Two 2½″ wide (instead of 5½″). Photo on page 60.

Use 42-44″ wide fabric. When strips appear in the cutting list, cut cross-grain strips (selvage to selvage).

	TWIN	DOUBLE/QUEEN	KING
Size width by height	56x40″	79x40″	90x40″
Number of 8″ Blocks	5	7	8

Yardage

Blocks			
Backgrounds – 2 lights	¼ yd. ea.	⅓ yd. ea.	⅓ yd. ea.
Star points – 2 darks	⅛ yd. ea.	¼ yd. ea.	¼ yd. ea.
Star centers – 2 lights	⅙ yd. ea.	⅙ yd. ea.	⅙ yd.
Applique – leaves	¼ yd.	⅓ yd.	½ yd.
stars	⅙ yd.	⅙ yd.	⅙ yd.
Setting triangles	½ yd.	¾ yd.	1 yd.
Pieced Border Dark	⅓ yd.	⅜ yd.	⅜ yd.
Pieced Border Light	⅓ yd.	½ yd.	½ yd.
Border 2	⅝ yd.	¾ yd.	⅞ yd.
Underlay	1⅛ yds.	1⅛ yds.	1½ yds.
Backing	2 yds.	2⅝ yds.	3 yds.
Binding	½ yd.	½ yd.	⅝ yd.

Cutting Patterns on page 50

For blocks	Twin	Double/Queen	King	
Background – 2⅞″ square	*20	*28	*32	*Cut these squares in half diagonally to make triangles.
2½″ square	20	28	32	
Star points – 2⅞″ square	*20	*28	*32	
Center – 4½″ square	5	7	8	**Cut these squares in quarters diagonally to make triangles.
Applique – leaves	16	24	28	
stars	5	7	8	
Setting triangles – 12½″ square	**2	**3	**4	
6½″ square	*2	*2	*2	
Border 1 Dark – 5¼″ square	**7	**10	**12	
Border 1 Light – 5¼″ square	**7	**10	**12	
2⅞″ square	*2	*2	*2	
Border 2 – 5½″ strips	3	4	5	
Binding – 2½″ strips	5	6	7	

Directions

Use ¼″ seam allowance throughout.

1. Piece blocks as shown.

2. Stitch blocks into a horizontal row with setting triangles. See diagram. Press.

3. Applique holly leaves and stars with your favorite method.

4. Prepare two borders of triangles as shown. Adjust to fit by taking up or letting out a few of the seams between units. Stitch to top and bottom of block row. Press.

5. Measure width of Topper. Prepare top and bottom borders 5½″ by width measurement. Stitch to top and bottom. Press.

6. Piece underlay with vertical seam(s). It should measure 15″ vertically and be the same width as your Topper. Stitch underlay to Topper.

7. Use your favorite layering, quilting, and binding methods to finish Topper.

For each block:

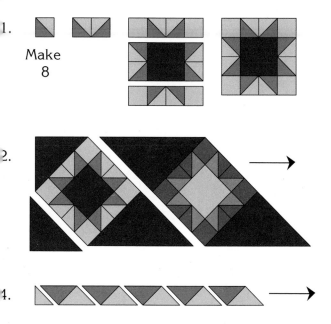

1. Make 8

2.

4.

Square Stars & Holly Topper—29″
For first border, cut eight dark 4⅛″ squares in quarters diagonally and nine light 4⅛″ squares in quarters diagonally. Cut outer border 2″ wide. Photo on page 24.

Scrappy Star Topper

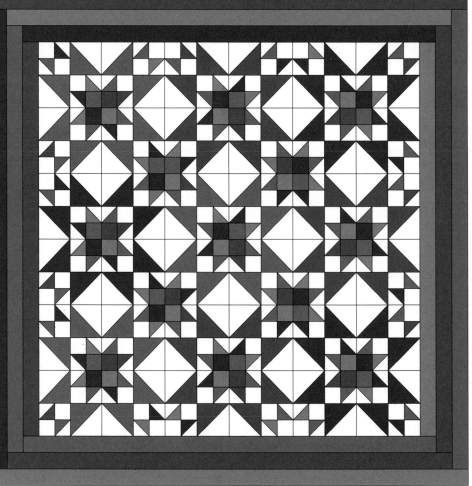

Photo on page 56. Use this Topper pattern for any size bed.

Use 42-44″ wide fabric. When strips appear in the cutting list, cut cross-grain strips (selvage to selvage).

Size	60″ square
Number of 16″ Blocks	9

Yardage

Blocks
Light scraps to total	2 yds.
Dark scraps to total	2 yds.
(scraps for 9 large stars at least 5½x21″)	
Borders – ⅓ yd. pieces	6
Backing	4 yds.
Binding	⅝ yd.

Cutting

Blocks
Lights – 4⅞″ squares	*36 each
Darks – 4⅞″ squares	*4 each from the large star fabrics
Lights & darks – 2⅞″ squares	*72 each
Lights – 2½″ squares	92
Darks – 2½″ squares	52
Borders – 2½″ strips	4 from each ⅓ yd.
Binding – 2½″ strips	7

*Cut these squares in half diagonally to make triangles.

42

Directions

Use ¼″ seam allowance throughout.

. Piece blocks as shown. One block has four dark corner squares. Four blocks have two dark and two light corner squares. Four blocks have one dark and three light corner squares.

. Stitch blocks into three horizontal rows. Block with four dark corners goes in the center. Blocks with three light corners go in the corners. Blocks with two dark and two light corners go on the sides. Rotate corner and side blocks using whole-quilt diagram as a guide; light corner squares go to outside edge of quilt. Stitch rows together. Press well.

. Measure height of Topper. Stitch two strips of the same fabric together for each side of Border 1, then trim to measured length. Stitch to sides of Topper. Press. Repeat for top and bottom of Border 1.

. Repeat Step 3 for Borders 2 and 3. Press well.

. Piece a 64″ square of backing.

. Use your favorite layering, quilting, and binding methods to finish Topper.

Make 144

Make 52

Make 20

Make 72

Make 16

Make 20

Make 1   Make 4   Make 4

20″ Pillow
Border made with leftover
strips from Topper border.
Photo on page 56.

Prairie Tulips Topper

Photo on page 52. Use this Topper pattern for any size bed.
Use 42-44″ wide fabric. When strips appear in the cutting list, cut cross-grain strips (selvage to selvage).

Size	48″ square
Number of 24″ Blocks	4

Yardage

Blocks
Light – background	1⅞ yds.
Dark – leaves, triangles	1 yd.
Medium 1 – tulips, triangles	⅝ yd.
Medium 2 – trapezoids, triangles	1 yd.
Backing	3½ yds.
Binding	½ yd.

Cutting Patterns on page 48

Light	6½″ square	4
	3⅞″ squares	*16
	12⅞″ squares	*8
Dark	leaf/stem applique	16
	5⅛″ squares	*16
Medium 1	tulip applique	16
	3⅞″ squares	*8
Medium 2	trapezoids	32
	3⅞″ squares	*8
Binding	2½″ strips	5

*Cut these squares in half diagonally to make triangles.

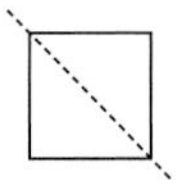

44

Directions

Use ¼″ seam allowance throughout.

1. Piece blocks as shown. Corner triangle unit made with two trapezoids and a triangle has a set-in point; stitch to seam intersection only, not to cut edges. Press well.

2. Applique tulips to corners using your favorite method.

3. Stitch blocks into two horizontal rows of two blocks. Stitch rows together. Press.

4. Piece a 52″ square of backing.

5. Use your favorite layering, quilting, and binding methods to finish Topper.

For each block:

Make 4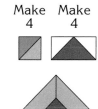

Make 4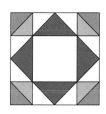

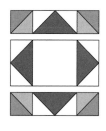

Make 4

24″ Pillow
Photo on page 52.

On Cloud Nine Topper

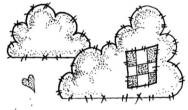

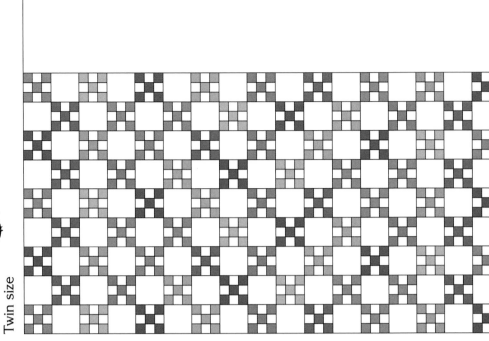

Twin size

Photo on page 49.

Use 42-44″ wide fabric. When strips appear in the cutting list, cut cross-grain strips (selvage to selvage).

	TWIN	DOUBLE/QUEEN	KING
Size width by height	51x40″	69x40″	87x40″
Number of 3″ Pieced Blocks	77	104	131

Yardage

Nine-patch darks			
⅙ yd. pieces (12 blocks ea.)	7	9	11
Nine-patch light, underlay,			
setting squares	2⅝ yds.	3⅛ yds.	4 yds.
Backing	1¾ yds.	2⅓ yds.	2⅞ yds.
Binding	½ yd.	½ yd.	⅝ yd.

Cutting

Dark strips for 9-patches			
1½″ strips from each fabric	3	3	3
Light strips for 9-patches			
1½″ strips	21	27	33
Setting squares – 3½″ squares	76	103	130
Binding – 2½″ strips	5	6	7

Directions

Use ¼″ seam allowance throughout.

1. Nine-patches

   a. Make 1 Strip Set A and 1 Strip Set B from **each** dark fabric (plus the one light background fabric).

   b. Press seam allowances of each Set A **out** from center, and seam allowances of each Set B **in** toward center.

   c. Crosscut into 1½″ segments (24 from A, 12 from B of each dark fabric).

   d. Stitch segments together as shown for each block. You will have twelve nine-patches from each dark fabric.

2. Distributing colors as desired, stitch blocks into horizontal rows, alternating with 3½″ setting squares of background fabric:

   - **Twin:** Odd rows start and end with nine-patches and have 9 nine-patches alternated with 8 background squares. Even rows start and end with background squares and have 8 nine-patches alternated with 9 background squares.

   - **Double/queen:** Odd rows start and end with nine-patches and have 12 nine-patches alternated with 11 background squares. Even rows start and end with background squares and have 11 nine-patches alternated with 12 background squares.

   - **King:** Odd rows start and end with nine-patches and have 15 nine-patches alternated with 14 background squares. Even rows start and end with background squares and have 14 nine-patches alternated with 15 background squares.

3. Press seam allowances of odd rows to right and seam allowances of even rows to left. Stitch rows together. Press well.

4. Piece underlay with vertical seam(s). It should measure 13½″ vertically and be the same width as your Topper. Stitch underlay to Topper.

5. Use your favorite layering, quilting, and binding methods to finish Topper.

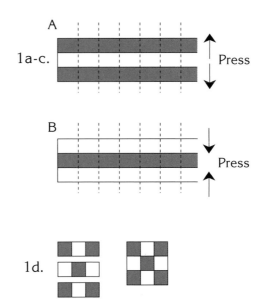

1a-c.

B

Press

1d.

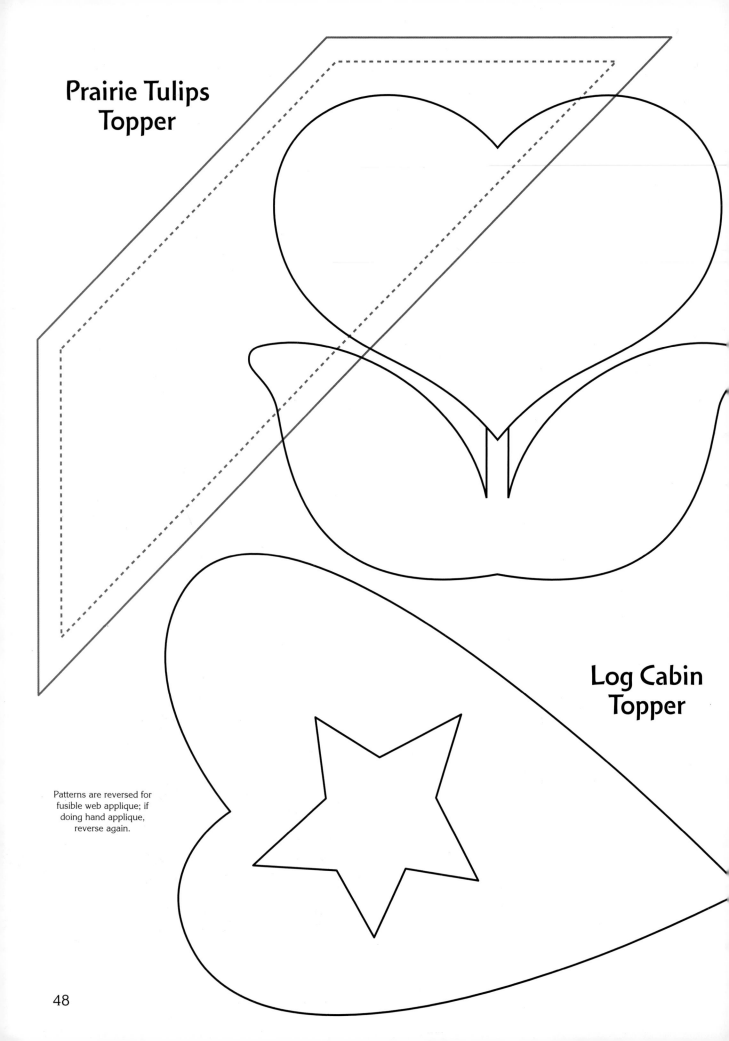

Prairie Tulips
Topper

Log Cabin
Topper

Patterns are reversed for
fusible web applique; if
doing hand applique,
reverse again.

Patterns are reversed for fusible web applique;
if doing hand applique, reverse again.

**Plaid Posies
Topper**

**Stars & Holly
Topper**

Celebration Topper

Patterns are reversed for fusible web applique; if doing hand applique, reverse again.

Applique the tulip across the top of a sheet and stencil a border on your wall to complete this bedroom ensemble. The square Prairie Tulips Topper would be beautiful draped over a round table.

Substitute any 15″ block in this Topper to create a totally new look. The small pillows feature cutouts of the large bouquet fabric. We fused it to a background square and machine appliqued around it. Then we quilted the background in a cross-hatched pattern.

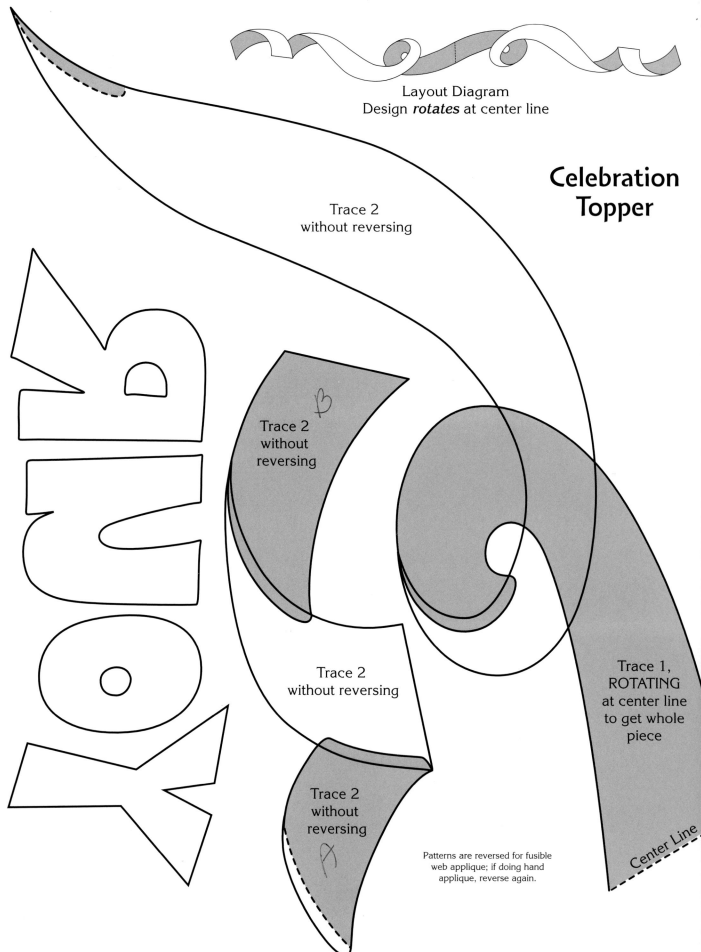

Layout Diagram
Design *rotates* at center line

Celebration Topper

Trace 2
without reversing

Trace 2
without
reversing

Trace 2
without reversing

Trace 2
without
reversing

Trace 1,
ROTATING
at center line
to get whole
piece

Center Line

Patterns are reversed for fusible
web applique; if doing hand
applique, reverse again.

Patterns are reversed for fusible
web applique; if doing hand
applique, reverse again.

Celebration
Topper

55

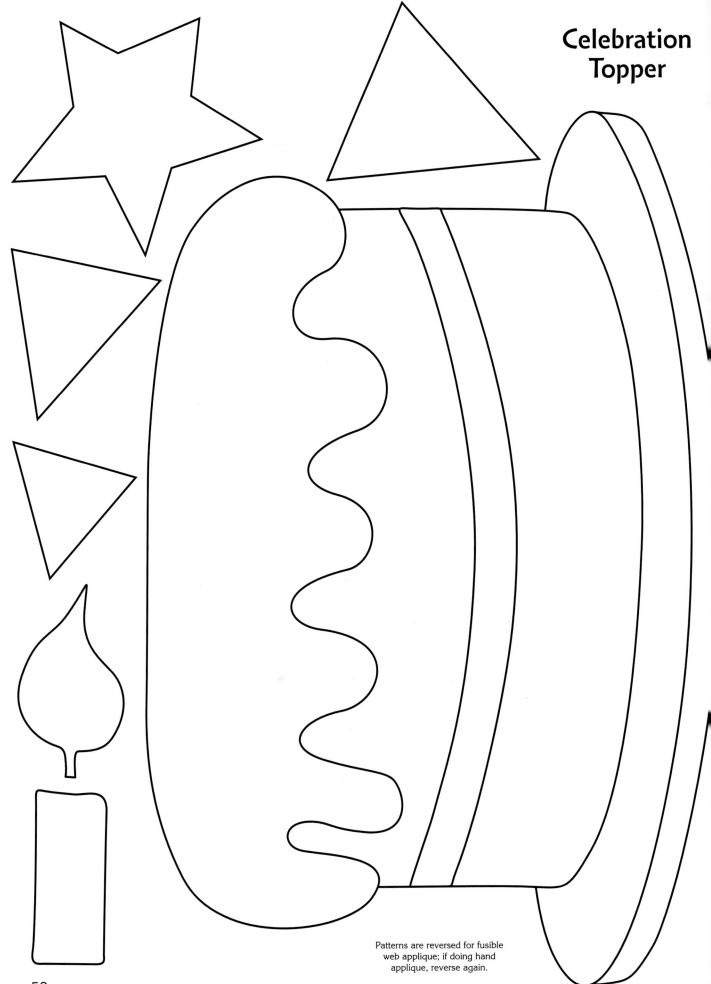

Celebration Topper

Patterns are reversed for fusible
web applique; if doing hand
applique, reverse again.

Celebration
Topper

Patterns are reversed for fusible
web applique; if doing hand
applique, reverse again.

Stars & Holly Table Runner

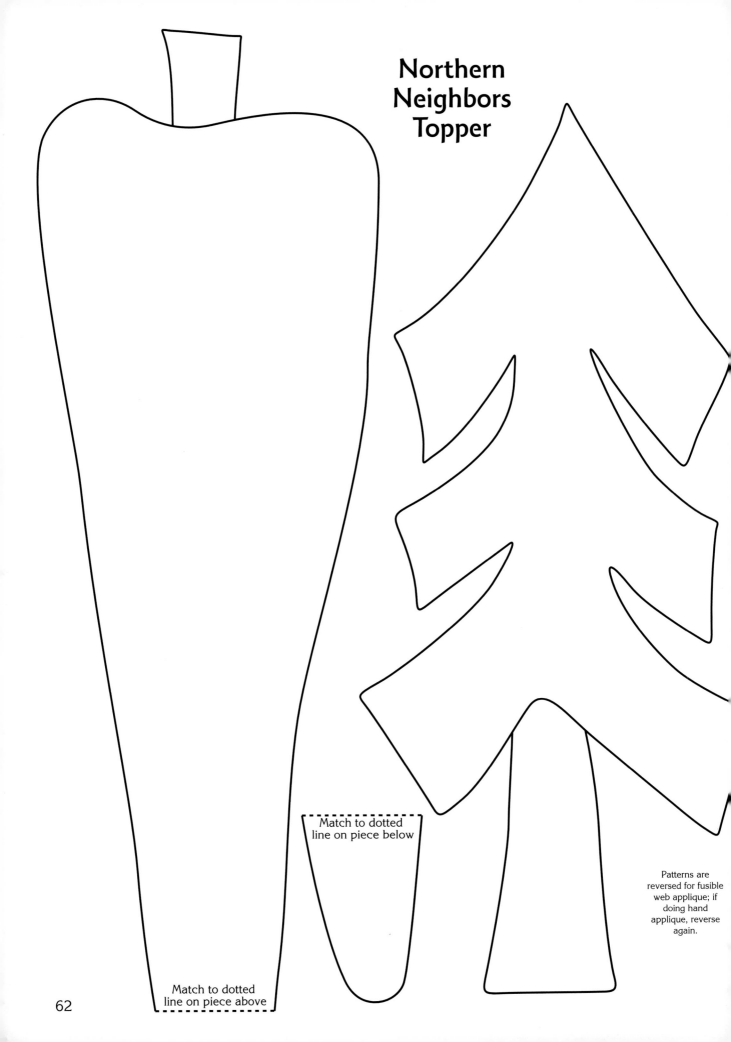

Northern Neighbors Topper

Match to dotted
line on piece below

Patterns are
reversed for fusible
web applique; if
doing hand
applique, reverse
again.

Match to dotted
line on piece above

Northern Neighbors Topper

Patterns are reversed for fusible web applique; if doing hand applique, reverse again.

Cozy up your family room with a fluffy "big square" quilt and this charming snowman Topper. Use it on a guest bed to warm the hearts of your visiting friends.

Northern Neighbors Topper

Patterns are reversed for fusible web applique; if doing hand applique, reverse again.

Patterns are reversed fo[r]
fusible web applique; i[f]
doing hand applique,
reverse again.

**Northern
Neighbors
Topper**

Northern Neighbors Topper

Patterns are reversed for fusible web applique; if doing hand applique, reverse again.

Northern Neighbors Topper

Patterns are reversed for fusible web applique; if doing hand applique, reverse again.

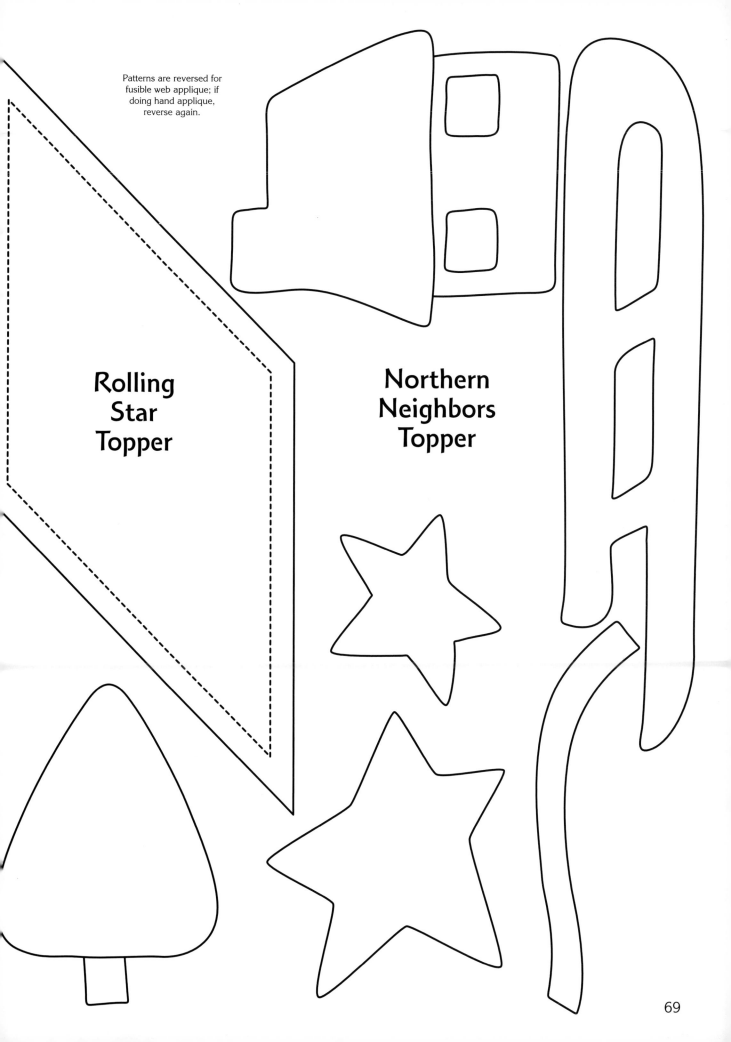

Patterns are reversed for fusible web applique; if doing hand applique, reverse again.

Rolling Star Topper

Northern Neighbors Topper

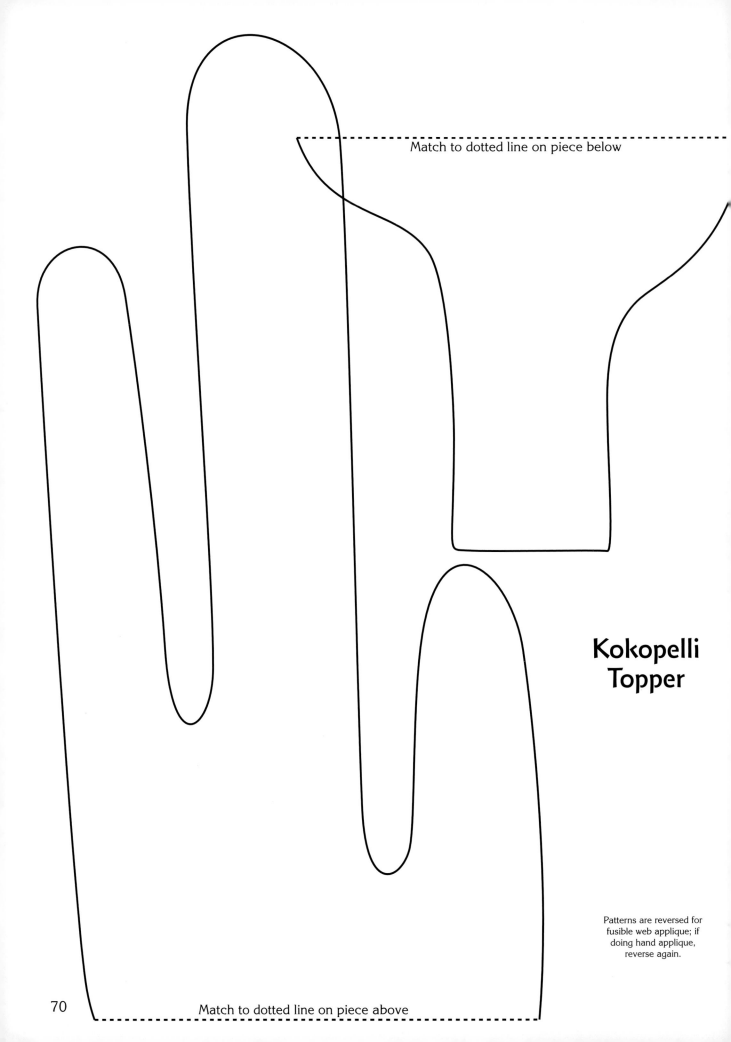

Match to dotted line on piece below

Kokopelli Topper

Patterns are reversed for
fusible web applique; if
doing hand applique,
reverse again.

Match to dotted line on piece above

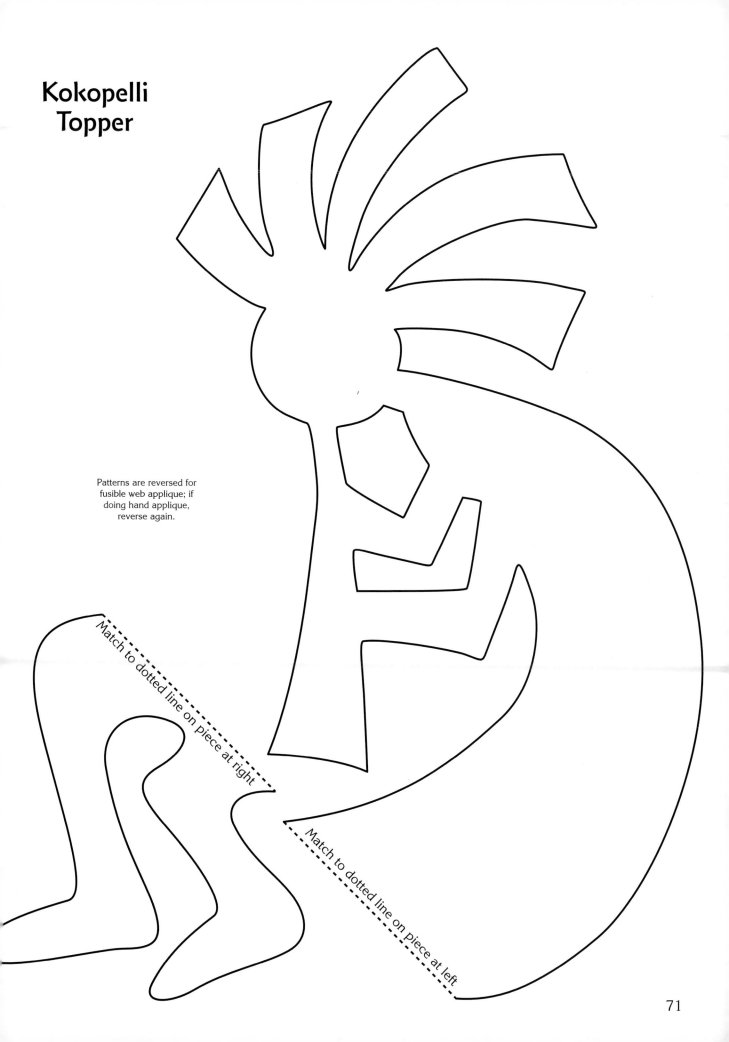

Kokopelli
Topper

Patterns are reversed for
fusible web applique; if
doing hand applique,
reverse again.

Match to dotted line on piece at right

Match to dotted line on piece at left

71

Northwoods Topper

Match to dotted line on tree top, page 73

Kokopelli Topper

Patterns are reversed for
fusible web applique; if
doing hand applique,
reverse again.

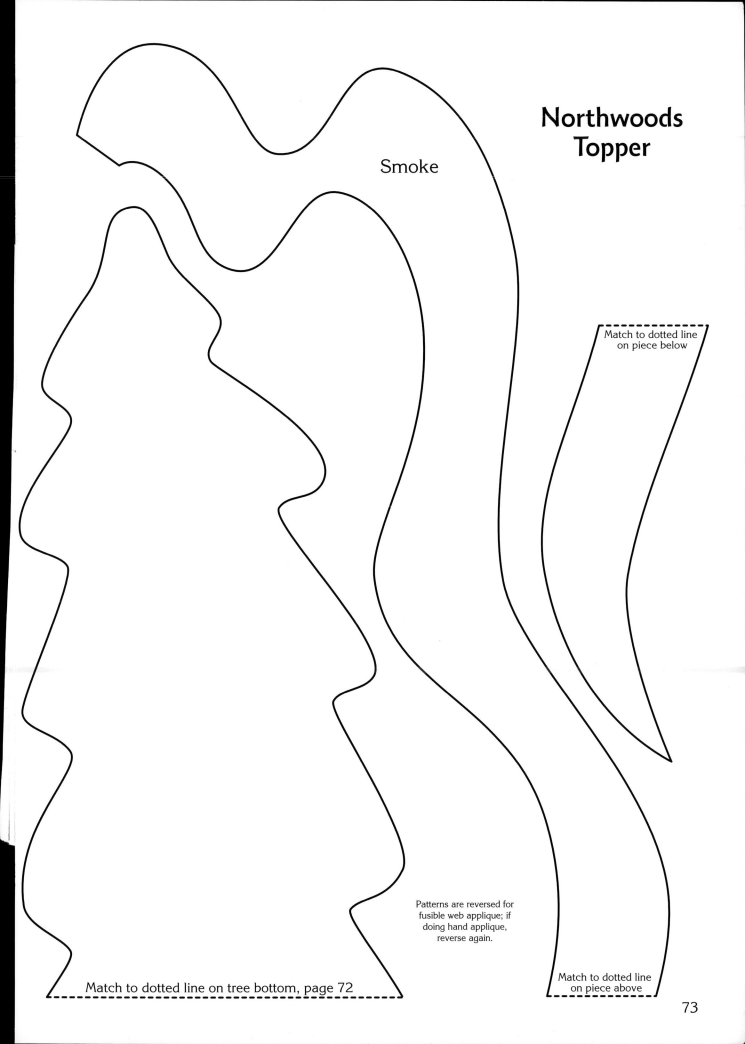

Smoke

Northwoods Topper

Match to dotted line
on piece below

Patterns are reversed for
fusible web applique; if
doing hand applique,
reverse again.

Match to dotted line on tree bottom, page 72

Match to dotted line
on piece above

Northwoods
Topper

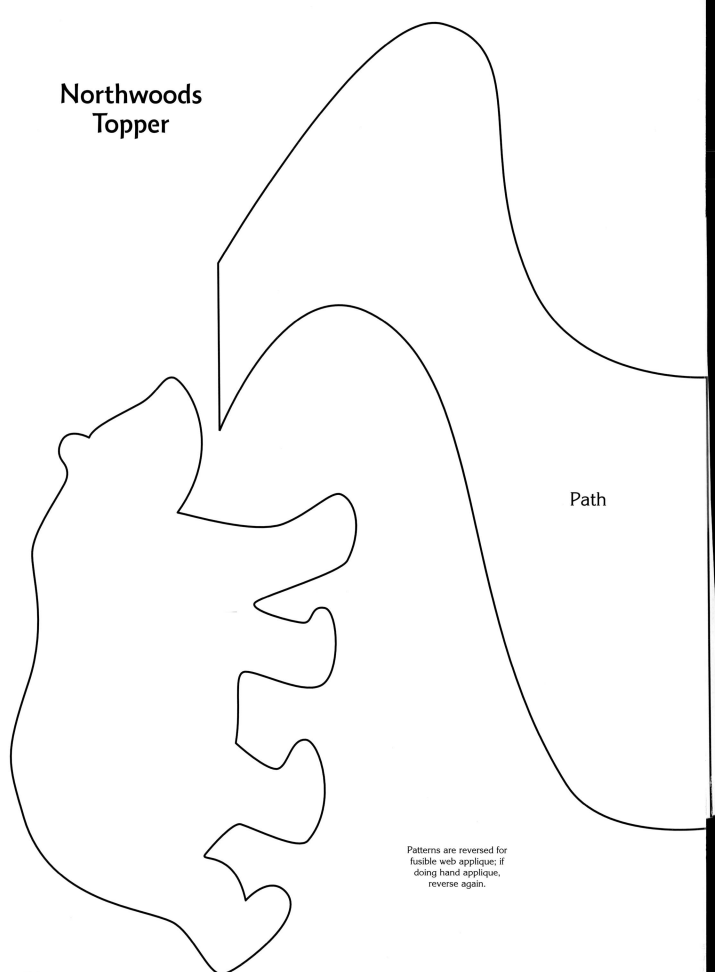

Path

Patterns are reversed for
fusible web applique; if
doing hand applique,
reverse again.

Northwoods Topper

Patterns are reversed for
fusible web applique; if
doing hand applique,
reverse again.

Northwoods
Topper

Northwoods
Topper

Patterns are reversed for
fusible web applique; if
doing hand applique,
reverse again.

Frosty Topper & Frosty Flannels Topper

Patterns are reversed
fusible web applique;
doing hand applique
reverse again.

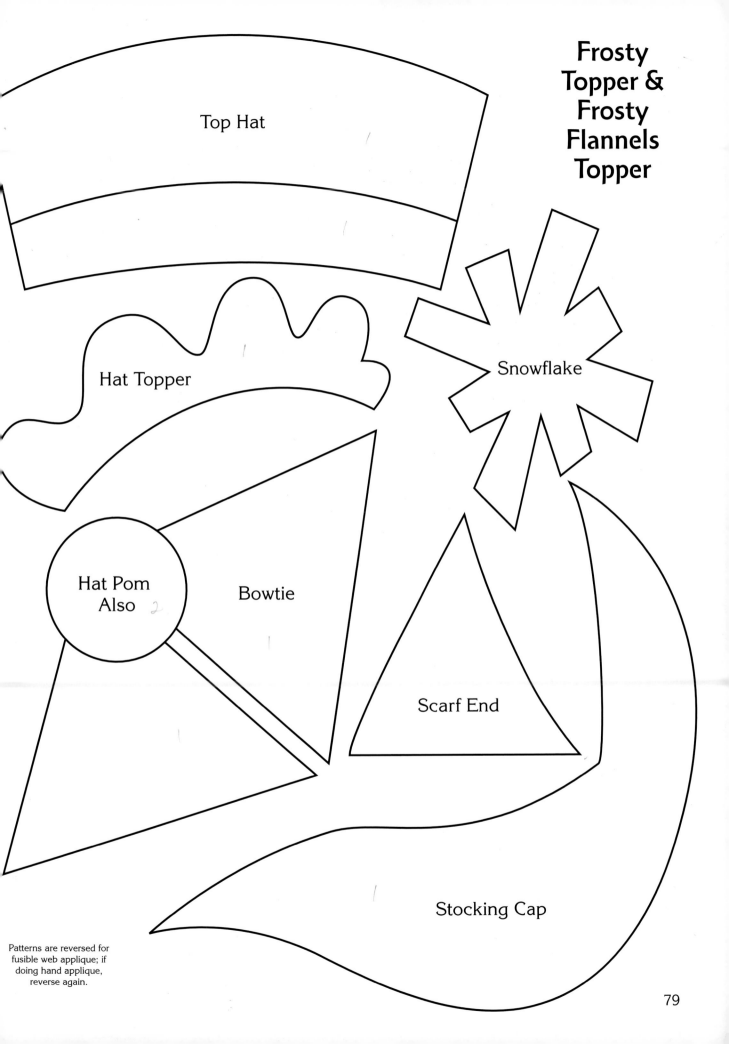

Top Hat

Snowflake

Hat Topper

Hat Pom
Also

Bowtie

Scarf End

Stocking Cap

Patterns are reversed for
fusible web applique; if
doing hand applique,
reverse again.

Creative Fabric Ideas from Possibilities®

Five Easy Pieces
Give your bedroom a designer look with these coordinating quilt projects. The quick & easy quilts feature the Sweet Bouquet Collection, a beautiful new line by Possibilities® for Peter Pan® Fabrics.

HouseWarmers
Nineteen quilts and 25 small projects for warming your home with the beauty of handmade quilts. Projects for every decor and skill level add personal touches to all the rooms in your house.

PHOTO MEMORIES IN FABRIC Series

Quilts and More
This informative book includes over 25 projects featuring photos transferred to fabric. Complete how-to instructions and full-sized patterns.

Album Coverups
Bring the fun and creativity of your memory book pages to the cover. Ten designs using fuse-and-use techniques personalize your projects.

P.S. I Love You Tw
Timeless projects mak cherished gifts. Yardag calculated for three sizes—little, crib, and t Complete directions ar multitude of technique including strip piecing paper-foundation piecing

P.S. I Love You
One of the top 10 quilting books in America, this book includes 17 quilts in cradle, crib, and twin sizes. Many nursery accessories for making darling children's rooms. Exceptional collection!

Time for a Chain
This is the only Irish Chain book you will ever need! Detailed cutting charts give measurements for single, double, and triple Irish Chains in five sizes. Rotary cutting for speed and accuracy.

T.L.C.
Tender Loving Covers
Another best seller! Eight heartwarming pictorial quilts for children and decorating are made by combining more than 50 blocks. Easy triangle method–Fast 45s.

Pillow Magic
Eight patchwork and applique blocks are made into pockets and attached to one pillow. Just turn them with the changing seasons! Includes an extra block and directions for a 50x50″ applique quilt.

Expresso Quil
Wake up and smell the coffee! Then make a q to wrap up in, or try a smaller project that ad flavor to a kitchen. Ste by-step directions for o 15 projects. Great coffe recipes coordinate with projects.

Snow Buddies
Snow people so charming you won't want to save them just for winter! Monthly patterns perfect for decorating your home. Fusible applique.

Here Comes Santa Claus
A magical Santa with an engaging northwoods flavor. Buttonhole stitching enhances his sprightly step. Great for beginners!

Pineapple Smoothy
From those who brought you *Pineapple Passion.* Template-free method is quick and accurate. Pineapple Rule helps guarantee perfect Pineapples.

Pineapple Rule
Sold separately

POSSIBILITIES®
...Publishers of DreamSpinners® patterns, I'll T Myself® sewing products, and Possibilities® boo

**Check with your local quilt sh
If not available, write or call us direc**

**8970 East Hampden Ave
Denver, Colorado 802
Orders only U.S. & Canada 1-800-474-20
303-740-6206 • Fax 303-220-74
www.possibilitiesquilt.c**